About the Author

As a boy I loved to sketch and paint and was encouraged to develop my art by my grandmother and her brother, Norman Mansbridge, the professional cartoonist and illustrator.

Whether at home in Cambridge (UK), travelling in Europe or further afield, in ministry and art, I find inspiration in the beauty of the details and character of the world around me. In watercolour, pen and ink or digital pencil and brush, I capture moments that stir the soul and freshen the spirit.

Edward B. Cearns
www.pocket-of-art.com

HEARTBREAK TO HEALING
PONDERINGS ON THE CAMINO

Edward B. Cearns

HEARTBREAK TO HEALING
PONDERINGS ON THE CAMINO

Vanguard Press

A CIP catalogue record for this title is
available from the British Library.

ISBN 978 1 80016 170 2

Vanguard Press is an imprint of
Pegasus Elliot MacKenzie Publishers Ltd.
www.pegasuspublishers.com

First Published in 2021

Vanguard Press
Sheraton House Castle Park
Cambridge England

Printed & Bound in Great Britain

Dedication

For every pilgrim on the Way
For every heart in need of healing

Acknowledgements

THANKS TO
My friends and family
The friends I met on this journey on the Camino
Medical and cardiac rehabilitation staff at Royal
Papworth Hospital and
Addenbrooke's Hospital, Cambridge.
My friends at Great St Mary's Church, Cambridge
Kerry McDermott-Lunn

PROLOGUE

The way of St. James

It was fairly early on the road from recovery from open heart surgery for an aortic aneurysm, that I decided that when I was strong enough, I would take another road: the world-famous Camino de Santiago de Compostela or 'Way to the tomb of the apostle St. James' in Northern Spain.

As I regained my physical and emotional strength in 2018, I felt that late summer/early autumn would be a good time to undertake such a spiritual and physical pilgrimage. As well as a journey of health, I had recently undertaken a journey of exploration for ministry within the Church, with a difficult outcome. So, I resolved that walking the Camino would be part of whatever happened next in my life.

This book is based on the journal I wrote every evening when walking part of the Camino de Santiago. In it, I share, as honestly as possible, my pilgrimage experience together with photos and my illustrations that they inspired.

My hope and prayer are that this little book will be of some help on your own journey.

Finding my way...

As is often my way in life, I first thought that I needed to approach walking the Camino in the most extreme way; in that I wanted to try and walk it all.

If you do not know, the whole of the Camino Francés—there are paths to Santiago that come from every direction in Europe and beyond—is seven hundred and seventy kilometres and begins in the Pyrenees...

When I tell you that it was only in late spring of 2018 that I really started to feel like myself again after heart surgery in January 2017, you will probably understand that it was with and through grace and humility that I revised my plan. Instead, I decided to walk the last one hundred kilometres to Santiago. (Pilgrims receive a certificate for walking at least one hundred kilometres of the Camino).

I started in Sarria, the common starting point for that stage of the Camino, which was a one hundred-and seventeen-kilometre journey.

Equally I realised that trying to carry my whole

pack was a challenge too much at that stage and so I opted to travel with a daypack and have the rest of my kit delivered from place to place.

Camino specialist travel companies was possibly going to be a bit ambitious for me. Accepting this with eventual grace, I developed a nine-day schedule instead, with help from 'Santiago Ways' one of the official tour operators, the Camino de Santiago. This schedule, allowing for about thirteen kilometres a day, would give me plenty of time for it to be much more than just an endurance test.

Of course, with factoring in the terrain—Galicia may not be a mountainous stage, but it is nevertheless pretty hilly (as I was to discover!)—and with the potential late summer heat, it would prove to be a challenge enough…

Finally, I should share that I opted to stay in modest hotels and guest houses rather than Albergue—pilgrims' hostels. To be honest, I've done my share of hostels and camping and as a number of friends pointed out, it would not be ideal for me to get sick (which happens from time to time in such shared living) whilst putting my body under the strain and stress of walking.

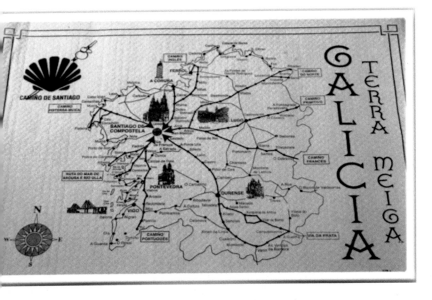

A placemat from Solento Pizza Restaurant in Sarria (where pizzas are the size of Galacia!) that shows the vastness of the Camino, was the location for my supper on the eve of my pilgrimage.

Day 1: Sarria to Ferreiros (13km)
"Hello, my name is Christian…"

I rose early and was on the path at first light; the autumnal mist was thick on the streets. Immediately I realised the popularity of the Camino as I joined a steady stream of pilgrims climbing the steps of the old town. As I left the town and descended into my first valley and crossed the beautiful medieval bridge, there was a rude interruption to the pastoral idyll as a high-speed train thundered past. I was reminded abruptly of the modernity of the pilgrims' way.

The steps of the old town

I survived my first day on the Camino. I promised myself that if I was going to share this very personal experience, I was going to be honest about it.

With that in mind, I'm crying as I write this. There are times today where I found it really tough, I had tears in my eyes, but I kept going;

immensely grateful that I did invest in some more trekking poles—the first having to be surrendered at the airport, before I even left the country.

Anyway, I digress... The first hill of the day was by far the steepest. I was blessed to share it with a lovely couple—Christian (no, I am really not making this up) and Catherine.

We shared some of our reasons for walking el Camino and after climbing the hill, Christian told me I needed to slow down, I was trying to go too fast and that I shouldn't be so tough on myself. I said I felt bad as they, like many, are walking the last one hundred kilometres to Santiago de Compostela in five days and I've opted to do it in twice that. Christian pointed out to me that it was enough that I was able to walk it and had chosen to.

Day 2: Ferreiros to Portomarín (9km)
Different ways, one day…

Well, my first experience of breakfast with other pilgrims has been in an enchanting old stone wall farmhouse and I had mixed feelings, as I tucked into my coffee and crusty bread, at what lay ahead of me.

Today proved to be very different from yesterday in many ways, as I was (mainly) descending towards a valley, the morning mist lingered for most of the journey, which made the early sunshine on the first stage all the more beautiful. Walking along I found myself singing quietly and the autumnal sunshine touching the landscape seemed to join in. I reflected on all that had passed over the last two years and the difficulty of the terrain gilded with glorious sunlight seemed appropriate.

Each day has its challenges; today it was regretting another coffee before walking and climbing down a ravine towards the end of the final descent. I was blessed to share the last stage today with a fun couple from upstate New York, one of whom had survived cancer (twice) and was taking photographic evidence to send to her sceptical children of what they descended today. This plucky pilgrim was today also overcoming vertigo as we walked along the enormous bridge into Portomarín. Just one of the countless examples of how 'The Way' helps us to face our fears as we move forward.

Day 3: Portomarin to Ventas de Narón (13km)
Some days…

Oh bother! I just wrote a long journal entry today and it has been lost to an iffy Wi-Fi connection. Let's just say it involved a reluctant suitcase; a hornet; lots of steep climbs; lots of people; (some very noisy); some deeply moving and spiritual pre-Roman ruins; a decision to go to the other café and the delight of meeting my New Yorker pilgrim friends from yesterday there; a blind chapel keeper and a friendly dog, currently sitting at my feet—the dog that is.

The door of the chapel of Magdalena, Ventas de Narón

Doorway of St Nicolas, Portomarin

Day 4: Ventas de Narón to Pala de Rei (12km)
Ministry and lemonade!

Today included waking up before the flies did (downside of rural living) and being shocked at how people rush past the things that make up the history of this walk and pilgrimage.

I was delighted today to have great conversations with a ministry to pilgrims over lemonade and rich tea, in a beautiful, converted farmhouse called La Fuente del Peregrino.

Later on, in the day's walking and after being fortified with delicious homemade apple pie, I took a five-kilometre detour to see the beautiful Monastery of Viladedonas, with great travel companions. It was a beautiful moment as the ancient columns of the church echoed to *Amazing Grace* played on Tom's fiddle.

The evening, though, was a less pleasant surprise when, after a round trip of three kilometres, at a communal meal in an auberge, I had the worst paella I have ever experienced!

The impressive entrance to Monastery of Viladedonas

Day 5: Palas de Rei to Melide (14km)
Ups and downs

Today was very much one of highs and lows—physically, spiritually and mentally. I slept well in a comfy bed but felt tired on the Camino in the morning.

It felt very much today that the cumulative impact had caught up with me. My body seems to have got wise to what I'm asking of it on a daily basis.

When I stopped at the first café after a few kilometres on the road out of town, I was delighted to be joined by Nancy and Tom from the day before and we were treated to some merriness on his travelling fiddle. Then we walked the rest of my day together.

Whilst the day started pretty chilly, the hot sultry Spanish sun came through much earlier than the last few days which made the walking much more difficult.

We passed through some absolutely beautiful scenery and talked politics, community, and church. Blessed by company and the shared experience.

Tom takes up the fiddle!

*Window of the
Church of Santa
Maria de Melide*

Crossing the stunning medieval bridge, we climbed the hill through the suburbs in the dusty heat to the pilgrimage town of Melide.

We had the traditional pilgrim food of octopus in Melide. Despite being a town a long way from the coast, the octopus travelled well and kept its freshness in medieval times.

On finding my hotel I completely crashed out. I was dehydrated and felt like the train I met on the path outside of Sarria on my first day had actually hit me.

I felt really bad for my Floridian companions as they had a further nine kilometres to go. I was delighted that they messaged me later to say that they had arrived safely.

I had little appetite in the evening for either food or even sharing much of the day's journey, and after only a few mouthfuls of very tasty dishes, I admitted defeat (most uncharacteristic of me).

Returning to the bar for the customary bottled water for tomorrow's journey, I ended up having a wonderful conversation with one of the family who owned the hotel.

Wise beyond his years, he said that the Camino is really a reflection of how people lead the rest of their life but some, if they are open to it, are changed by the experience.

Time after time on this journey I have been so touched that by trusting and being open, God and the Way has provided.

Whilst my feet may be sore and my legs may ache, my soul is definitely lighter this evening.

It is a journey that is as much about going deeper into the heart of God, as it is about moving forward in our own lives.

To me it seems to be about active trust, submitting but in action, stillness in walking and love in demonstration.

The Pellegrino's Shadow

Day 6: Melide to Arzúa (14km)
Let it flow; let it go

Melide was enveloped in a veil of mist this morning and as I set off with a little more spring in my step, I suddenly felt a little homesick for Cambridge as I passed the Sunday markets setting up.

I was blessed this morning with some time to walk alone. There were definitely fewer pilgrims around—those walking great distances tend to leave before I wake, and others still were resting today.

In the relative solitude I found the walking through the woodlands profoundly moving today. The delights of woodland treasure—bejewelled cobwebs, colourful fungus and paths—would not be out of place in a J.R.R. Tolkien adaptation. I listened to music, including the Christian vocalist Steve Green. I have always enjoyed his musical style that is somewhere between musical theatre and devotional. It served only to heighten the mood.

There is something incredibly potent about placing one's boots on the same path as millions of pilgrims before. Wherever we come from, whatever we bring, there is space on the path for us.

The lone walker

This afternoon I was blessed to catch up with two lovely Mexican sisters who are on the same itinerary as myself, María and Selina. We walked and talked. Maria asked what brought me here and I shared something of my story.

As we were about to enter a village on the woodland path there was the sound of bagpipes (the Celtic culture is big here) and a singer. Maria turned to me to translate the Spanish song. "The water that you can't drink, let it go, let it flow away.

The path takes many forms....

My Pilgrim sisters!

Day 7: Arzúa to Salceda (11km)
Crossroads

This morning was an enchanting intertwining of autumn mist and sunlight. It was an artist or photographer's delight.

I have been completely surprised by the beauty on this walk. It has been so full of treasures.

As I was walking through beautiful woodland today, I reached a crossroads; at this point the Camino was clearly marked with one of the very regular stones with a yellow arrow and the exact kilometres and metres left till we reached Santiago.

I have also observed that as we get closer to Santiago, there are often more paths other than the Camino to choose from.

I often find as an artist that the best way to present a scene is to be some distance from it, to give it some perspective. In the case of the crossroads, of course, this meant stepping off the Camino and walking a little way down another path to create the view looking back.

As I was doing this a couple of travellers on the Camino called out, clearly concerned I was wandering off in entirely the wrong direction

I explained that I was taking a photo of the crossroads which I proceeded to do, of course now having them in the frame.

What I realised then was that whilst markers on the path are helpful, what is more meaningful is a fellow traveller walking that path with us giving context and vitality.

Day 8: Salceda to Lavacolla (22km)
Woodland wonders

Goodness, what a day! One of my longest on the Camino, of twenty-two kilometres. It involved close encounters with speeding lorries in the rain (thankfully it was only my hat that blew off in the backdraft). It is less than ideal, that the Camino at times takes the pilgrim along the side of a motorway—it was terrifying!

Lovely conversations; prayer; time; music; and, as with every day on the Camino for me, some tears as well.

I woke up to a very active mist today, mizzle, the kind that gets you pretty wet without you realising.

I was incredibly grateful for the waterproof and backpack cover I had been carrying for the last one hundred kilometres. In fact, I was rather grateful for the rain itself. It brought out the scents of the woodland: pine and eucalyptus and earth mingled — it was glorious.

There were more examples of the Camino spirit today. I entered a café—probably looking somewhat bedraggled—and after ordering a cold drink I went in search of the stamp for my pilgrim's passport. When I turned back to my drink there was a slice of unordered Spanish omelette. On checking with the young smiley chap who had served me he said, 'Yes, it's free, for you. You need energy.'

I can hardly believe that, God willing, tomorrow night I will be in Santiago. What an extraordinary journey: beautiful people, beautiful scenery, time with God, with His creation and with oneself.

Today was nicely rounded off by joining my fellow pilgrims for a meal, sharing the adventures of our day, our experiences—the ups and the downs.

I think my prayer tonight is that we all try to live the Way a little better: with generosity, gratefulness, and grace.

Day 9: Lavacolla to Santiago de Compostela
(10km)
Glory comes in many forms

The day started early: I woke up at six a.m. in anticipation of what lay ahead and decided to get my kit together.

I considered leaving before breakfast but, partly as I felt I had used up a few of my nine lives crossing the national roads on the day before, and partly because I thought it would be good to walk into Santiago with my fellow pilgrim friends, I decided to wait and take on some fuel for the day at breakfast. I am so glad I made that decision.

The impressive sculpture at Monte Gozo

Whilst a pilgrimage is a personal one, it thrives within the company and context of others.

As our guesthouse was a few kilometres from the start, I worked out a route to re-join it. What a joy to be on the road early enough to witness the sunrise and to share it with others.

We arrived at the halfway point in good time, Monte Gozo—the Mount of Joy—so called as it is the first point on the journey that the pilgrim sees the destination, the Cathedral of Saint James. We climbed up to the stunning sculpture, built to commemorate Pope John Paul II's visit. It was only after the journey's end that I realised that we had not visited the famous Pilgrim Sentinels further up the hill.

However, we did visit the chapel of San Marco; not for the first time on the journey I felt a little like a knight of old laying his sword/trekking poles down in the pew next to him to pray for the battle that lay ahead.

With God's grace, gosh what battles I have faced: the decision of elective heart surgery, going through with it and the recovery along with coming to terms with the complexity of following one's vocation. Now I was about to complete a one hundred- and eighteen-kilometre journey through the hills of Northern Spain to the tomb of one of Jesus' first followers.

Through it all—all the uncertainty, all the worry and fear and doubt—I have felt Christ's light guiding, and that I have been held in love and prayer by family and friends. How fitting then that when I asked Maria where the votive candles were at the chapel she said, 'I've already lit one for you, and for your journey ahead.'

Now I felt the pilgrim's joy (I believe I said "Wow!") as I spotted the impressive edifice of Santiago Cathedral as I climbed the Mound to the stunning sculpture ahead of our final stage.

A few kilometres later, as we entered the city, I was reminded once again how difficult it was to be a pilgrim. Firstly, as I grew ever nearer the cathedral disappeared completely behind the last hill and only became visible again when we were mere hundreds of metres away.

Secondly, how out of place we looked in a regional capital, now that pilgrims were the minority, and the Camino signs themselves were much harder to discern amongst the street furniture of the urban landscape, and many of the locals looked on at us with a mixture of pity and irritation.

Nevertheless, we found our way to the beautiful historical quarter and entered the archway into the famous Obradoiro Square.

Whilst I did of course see the stunning cathedral, my eye was also drawn to one of those tourists' 'trains' that was parked right against the building's facade—I felt God's sense of humour again…

I also realised I was myself a tourist attraction when a visitor asked if she could take my photo. I guess I did look the part, with trekking poles, grizzly beard, (I will be trimming it) and calves even bigger than when I started.

After an afternoon of queuing for my certificate and chatting with fellow pilgrims and then the extra kilometres and adventure of finding my hotels (a little local difficulty involved relocating) I joined my friends for the evening Pilgrim's Mass.

I am not sure quite what I expected to find in the interior of the cathedral, but I was honestly shocked by the towering gold and rather chilly looking angels.

I did indeed hug the apostle, but felt much more emotion in the quiet of the small and blissfully relatively modest crypt.

Again, with honesty, I felt somewhat saddened by the service and became visibly moved towards the end. Whilst I understand that it is a Spanish cathedral, it is also the centre of an international pilgrimage; the service was presented as a Pilgrims Mass. So, it seemed strange to me, to give an eloquent and passionate twenty-minute sermon in a language (and I do not mean theology) that half of the congregation did not understand. I am sure it would be possible to at least provide a precise if not a complete translation.

My point was made all the more poignant when my Spanish speaking friends explained to me afterwards that his whole homily was about the importance of approaching God in his humanity as well as his divinity...

Having journeyed the Camino, it spoke of the sadness to me of the wider church, that I was unable to take part in communion.

God, I have found on the journey of faith, is

always one of surprises. I certainly was not expecting to find the beauty of the Camino mostly in the beauty of the countryside and the love and faith of those I met along and travelled with, on the path.

I suppose He is reminding me that the destination was never just a physical place, but a deeper understanding and peace with ourselves and Him and with healed hearts to be better or less imperfect ministers of His love and grace as we journey forward.

'Travellers. There is no path, paths are made by walking'

Just one of the many tables of hospitality along the Camino

This was not my idea!

Sights and Treasures Along the Way...

Cows in the barn in Ligonde

Old barn door

Aging tractors in the farmyard

Grain Store outside of Portomarin

Santiago de Compostela Cathedral

*Good morning
Ewe!*

*St Cristoria's Church Bell
Tower at Arzúa*

Woodland Vista

Backpack and Trekking Poles